W9-BBJ-630

WILD WHEELS!

Hottest Dragsters and Funny Cars

By Jim Gigliotti

Enslow Publishers, Inc.
40 Industrial Road
Box 398
Berkeley Heights, NJ 07922
USA
http://www.enslow.com

Library of Congress Cataloging-in-Publication Data

Gigliotti, Jim.
  Hottest dragsters and funny cars / by Jim Gigliotti.
    p. cm. — (Wild wheels!)
  Summary: "Learn about drag racing, funny cars, and experience what it
feels like to spend the day at a drag race"—Provided by publisher.
  Includes bibliographical references and index.
  ISBN-13: 978-0-7660-2870-8
  ISBN-10: 0-7660-2870-4
  1. Drag racing—Juvenile literature. 2. Dragsters—Juvenile
literature. I. Title.
  GV1029.3.G54 2008
  796.72—dc22

                                2007007424

Printed in the United States of America

10 9 8 7 6 5 4 3 2 1

To Our Readers:
We have done our best to make sure that all Internet Addresses in this book were
active and appropriate when we went to press. However, the author and publisher have
no control over and assume no liability for the material available on those Internet sites
or on other Web sites they may link to. Any comments or suggestions can be sent by
e-mail to comments@enslow.com or to the address on the back cover.

Cover photo: Auto Imagery **Back cover:** Auto Imagery
Photo Credits: Alamy/Wesley Hitt, p. 25; Associated Press, p. 34; AP/Frank Bowman,
pp. 1, 7; AP/Greg Griffo, pp. 3, 18; AP/Jack Dempsy, p. 17; AP/Ken Sklute, p. 33;
AP/Steve Kohls, pp. 4–5; Auto Imagery, pp. 1, 3, 8, 13, 14, 15, 19, 20 (all), 22, 23, 24,
26–27, 27, 28, 29, 30, 35, 36–37, 40, 42 (both), 44; Getty Images/Jamie Squire, p. 9;
iStockPhoto, p. 38.

Contents

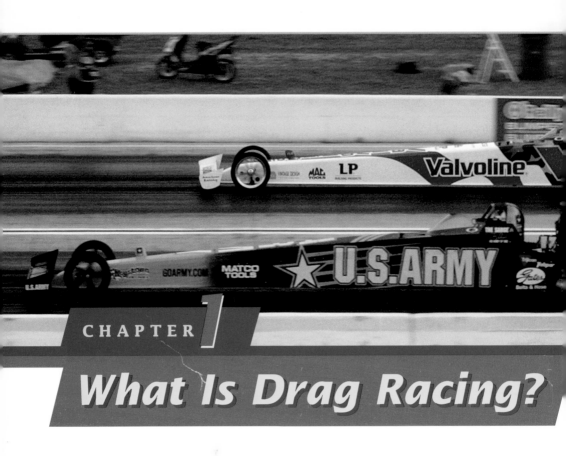

CHAPTER 1

What Is Drag Racing?

It is a hot day at a long, thin racetrack in Pomona, in Southern California. Two of the fastest vehicles on Earth are ready to sprint side-by-side down a quarter-mile track. They are Top Fuel dragsters competing at the famous Winternationals drag-racing event in 2006. Flames shoot out of the headers, or exhaust pipes, of one of the dragsters as they rumble at the starting line.

The engines roar. The ground shakes. The starting lights count down. As the green

lights appear, so does a cloud of smoke, with an ear-splitting crack— and they're off! The two cars are a blur as they power down the track. The race is over in a few seconds, but the powerful machines reached as much as 330 miles per hour (mph)!

The fans cheer wildly. The dragster driven by fan favorite Melanie Troxel crosses the finish line just in front of her rival Tony Schumacher. The race is so close that only the most high-tech equipment can prove that Troxel's car has finished ahead of Schumacher's by less than a second.

It is a scene like no other in American sports. A drag-racing meet is a whirlwind of colors, sights, and sounds. It takes just a few seconds for the fastest racers to zoom down the track and cross the finish line. But drag racing is a lot more than just the five or six seconds of the race. The drivers of drag racing have a passion for racing cars.

The History of Drag Racing

Experts generally agree that modern drag racing began in Southern California in the late 1940s and early 1950s. The dry bed of the Los Angeles River was one place owners raced their cars. The cars were called hot rods, and were "souped-up." That means that the cars' engines were faster and more powerful than those in regular cars. The hot rods raced side-by-side on a straight track.

Those races were illegal—not to mention dangerous. But in 1951, the National Hot Rod Association (NHRA) was formed. The NHRA began working to find places for drivers to race that were safer and legal. Soon, tracks opened in places such as Santa Ana, California, and Pomona, California. The NHRA made up rules for drag racing.

In the 1950s and 1960s, television began bringing drag racing into Americans' living rooms. This helped it to grow in popularity. By the 1970s, the sport had a huge following.

A "starter" leaps into the air waving a flag to signal the start of a drag race in Florida in 1954.

Racers such as Don Prudhomme, Don Garlits, and Shirley Muldowney became famous. Today, drivers including Tony Schumacher, John Force, Melanie Troxel, and more carry on the tradition.

Types of Drag Racing

There are three main types of drag racing: Top Fuel, Funny Car, and Pro Stock. Top Fuel dragsters are long and thin. They are the fastest of all the drag racing cars. Funny Cars and Pro Stock cars look more like regular cars.

Professional NHRA drivers compete in these categories, plus Pro Stock Motorcycle. Professionals, or "pros," are people who make money performing a certain skill—in this case, drag racing.

In addition to earning money, pro drivers earn points for where they finish at each racing event during the season. At the end of the season, the driver with the most points wins the championship. There is a champion for each type of drag racing.

The Basics

A drag race is a competition between two vehicles. The object is to see which of the two can cover a short, straight distance,

Ron Capps burns rubber in his Funny Car to get ready for a race in Atlanta, Georgia, in 2006.

O, Christmas Tree

A pole of colorful starting lights tells the drivers when a race is about to start. This signal pole is called the "Christmas Tree" for its bright colors. The tree is located between the two racers in the center of the track.

As the drivers approach the starting line, the top row of yellow lights comes on. Then the cars inch forward to touch the line. That is when the second row of yellow lights comes on. Soon, the next three rows light up. The drivers know the race is about to start!

When the two green lights near the bottom of the tree light up, it is time to put the pedal to the metal. Jumping off the starting line at the green lights is a big part of winning a race. If the driver waits too long, his or her opponent gets a head start. But if the driver goes too soon, a red light at the bottom will signal a foul. That means the driver is disqualified and has to leave the race.

starting from a standstill, in the shortest amount of time. The distance is usually a quarter of a mile. That is the same as one lap around a regulation running track, or almost four-and-a-half football fields long. The first drag racer to cross the finish line wins.

Racers compete against each other in drag meets. First, they make qualifying runs. During the qualifying runs, drivers are competing against the clock and not against each other. Qualifying runs are made to decide the 16 racers who have the lowest elapsed time. Elapsed time (ET)

WILD
FACT

Drag racing cars are very expensive to build. Plus, it takes a team of mechanics to take care of each dragster. Because of this, every professional driver needs sponsors. Sponsors help pay the costs of racing a dragster. Sponsors are usually big companies that want to advertise their products to racing fans. They pay to put their company logos on the cars and racing gear of the team they sponsor. That advertising is seen by everyone watching the race.

What's in a Name?

Drag racing is one of the world's most colorful sports. Its stars have had some colorful nicknames, too. Don Garlits, one of the most famous drag racers ever, was called "Big Daddy" by an announcer at the U.S. Nationals in 1962. The nickname stuck.

Funny Car star Don Prudhomme was called "The Snake" because of his lightning–quick starts. Tom McEwen was one of Prudhomme's top rivals. He was called "The Mongoose" because that is one of the few animals that can beat a snake in battle.

Lots of other stars had nicknames, too. Shirley Muldowney was called "Cha–Cha." Ed McCulloch was "Ace." And Tommy Ivo was called "T.V. Tommy" because he was one of the original Mouseketeers on the popular *Mickey Mouse Club* television show in the 1950s.

is the total time the run takes from start to finish.

The 16 qualifiers are then paired one-against-one in elimination races. After one round, the field is left with eight winners. After the next round, there are four drivers left. And then there are only two. Those two drivers race against each other in the finals. The winner of that race is the champion of the drag meet. Some of the elimination

races are so close that times are computed to one one-thousandth of a second!

It seems simple. The fastest car will have the lowest elapsed time and end up winning the race—right? Not necessarily. It is possible for the winner of an elimination race to have a higher ET. It depends on how the driver handles the car on the track. ET is not a factor in an elimination-round victory, but it is still an important concept for drivers. When a driver wins an elimination round with a higher ET than his or her competitor, it is called a "holeshot" victory.

SAFETY FIRST—AND ALWAYS!

Operating any vehicle at high speeds is DANGEROUS. Special training and safety equipment are needed for racing. The drivers you see at the track and on television, or that you read about, have many years of experience. They use the most modern safety equipment. Their vehicles are built and taken care of according to NHRA rules.

Even with all of these precautions, drag racing is still dangerous for experienced drivers. On March 19, 2007, Funny Car driver Eric Medlen was critically injured in a crash during a practice run in Gainesville, Florida. Tragically, he died four days later. Do not try drag racing. Leave it to the professionals.

As a Top Fuel dragster sprints off the starting line, its engine creates a deafening roar. Burning fuel creates a blinding fireball.

CHAPTER 2

Top Fuel Dragsters

Top Fuel cars are the fastest of all the drag racing cars. They can reach speeds of more than 300 mph. It can take them as little as four-and-a-half seconds to cover a quarter-mile drag race track. Do not blink— or you might miss the race!

These dragsters are instantly recognizable by their long, thin frames. How long are they? A Top Fuel dragster's wheelbase is 285 to 300 inches—that is up to 25 feet long! Compare that with the wheelbase of a typical passenger car, which is around 110 inches—just over

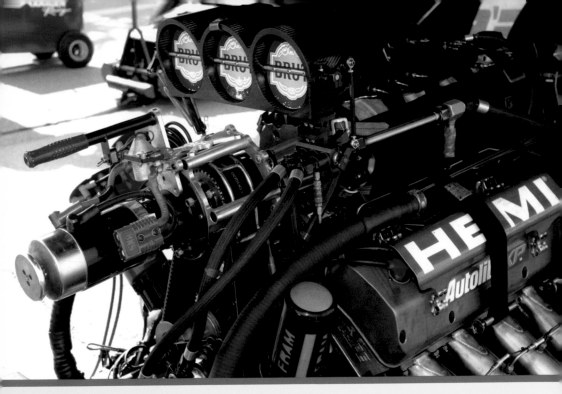

Top Fuel dragsters and Funny Cars have almost identical engines. These all-aluminum powerhouses cost about $50,000 to build.

nine feet. (Wheelbase is the distance between the center of the front wheel and the center of the rear wheel.) Top Fuel dragsters are only a few feet high except for a tall wing on the back. The wing is designed to direct air currents for faster performance.

A Top Fuel dragster's engine is at the back of the vehicle for the driver's safety. This way, if something goes wrong with the engine, the problem stays behind the driver.

Every Top Fuel dragster has a small wheelie bar on its back end. A "wheelie" is when the front end of a car lifts off the ground and the car balances on its back wheels. Top Fuel dragsters go at such high speeds and are so heavy in the back that they can easily wheelie, and possibly flip over. The wheelie bar keeps the front end from lifting too far off the ground.

These amazing vehicles do not run on regular gasoline. Instead, they run on a fuel called nitromethane, sometimes called "nitro." It is much more powerful than regular gasoline. In fact, nitromethane has even been used for rocket fuel.

Top Fuel dragsters are so powerful that they can accelerate, or increase their

Shirley "Cha-Cha" Muldowney is a Top Fuel drag racing legend. She raced in the 1970s and 1980s.

speed, faster than a fighter jet. Some Top Fuel dragsters can have more than 6,000 horsepower (hp) in their engines. Horsepower is a measure of engine performance. It compares the power created by one horse to what an engine can do. This means it would take 6,000 horses working together to produce enough power to drive a Top Fuel

WILD FACT

Top Fuel driver Don Garlits might be the most legendary drag racer ever. In 2001, the NHRA celebrated its 50th anniversary by naming the top 50 drivers of all time. Garlits was number one on the list.

dragster at top speed! A regular passenger car has around 150 hp. A Top Fuel dragster has more than 40 times more power!

Top Fuel dragsters beat the world's fastest sports cars, too. For example, the Porsche Carrera GT can accelerate from zero to 60 mph in about 3.8 seconds. But the

The tires on a Top Fuel dragster are called "slicks." That is because they do not have any treads. The treads on a regular car's tires are the grooves that help them better grip the road. But for a Top Fuel dragster, "no grooves" means that more of the tire hits the road. And that means the tire can pull the dragster along faster.

The back tires of a Top Fuel dragster are about 18 inches wide and about 118 inches around. The front tires are much smaller, the size of airplane or bike tires.

Top Fuel drag racing is tough on tires! The cars' high speeds create high temperatures, which wear the tires out quickly. The large back tires usually last only about four to six drag racing runs. Compare that with the life of regular car tires. Most of those can last as many as 40,000 to 50,000 miles. Four to six runs for a dragster is only one to one and a half miles!

Drag racing star Melanie Troxel poses with a Top Fuel dragster's large rear tire.

17

fastest Top Fuel cars can reach 100 mph in only eight-tenths of a second!

The World's Fastest

The current record holder for speed in a Top Fuel dragster is Tony Schumacher. In 2005, he reached a top speed of 337.58 mph during a race in Brainerd, Minnesota.

According to the NHRA, the quickest that a Top Fuel dragster has covered a quarter mile is 4.428 seconds. Schumacher set that elapsed time world record on November 12, 2006. He did it while

Tony Schumacher is one of the best Top Fuel drivers around. Here, he celebrates his 2004 U.S. Nationals victory.

Hanging Out the Laundry

Speeds of more than 300 mph are too fast for brakes alone to slow down a dragster on a quarter-mile track. So when a driver crosses the finish line, he or she pulls a lever inside the car to release a parachute from the back of the car. This is known as "hanging out the laundry."

The parachute acts as a powerful "brake." When the car has slowed down enough, the driver can then stop it using the regular brakes. If a driver releases the parachute too late, or the parachute does not work properly, the car slides into a giant sand pit at the end of the drag strip. The sand helps to stop the car safely.

competing against Melanie Troxel in the finals of an event at Pomona, California.

Many feel that Schumacher is the best Top Fuel driver today. In 2006, he won Top Fuel's overall season points championship for the third year in a row and for the fourth time in his career.

Drag Racing Cars vs. Sports Cars

Tony Schumacher's 2005 Hadman R.E.D. Top Fuel Dragster

John Force's 2004 Ford Funny Car

Greg Anderson's 2005 Pontiac Grand Am Pro Stock Car

Even the hottest, fastest sports cars in the world cannot stand up to the fastest drag racing cars. So when it comes to regular passenger cars, forget it! Drag racing cars leave them in the dust.

DRAG RACING CARS	TOP SPEED (MPH)
Hadman R.E.D. Top Fuel Dragster	336.15
Ford Funny Car	333.58
Pontiac Grand Am Pro Stock Car	208.23
Harley-Davidson V-Rod Pro Stock Motorcycle	197.45

SPORTS CARS	TOP SPEED (MPH)
Saleen S7 Twin Turbo	260
Ultima Can-Am 640 & GTR 640	231
Mercedes-Benz SLR McLaren	207
Ford GT	205
Lamborghini Murciélago	205
Porsche Carrera GT	205

Tony Bartone's Funny Car is a Chevrolet Monte Carlo tricked out for racing. All Funny Cars are based on regular passenger car models.

CHAPTER 3

Funny Cars

Funny Cars got their name because they look like regular cars—sort of. But when you look closer, they seem a little "funny." First of all, there are no doors. And there is no passenger seat or back seat. Also, the entire body of the car lifts up so mechanics can work on the engine. In fact, a Funny Car driver gets in and out of the car when the body is lifted up.

If there is an emergency during a race, though, he or she can open up an escape hatch (door) in the roof. Like Top Fuel dragsters, Funny Cars run on a fuel mixture made up mostly of nitromethane. Unlike a Top Fuel dragster, though, a Funny Car's engine is at the front of the car.

Funny Cars do not go as fast as Top Fuel dragsters, but they are not too far behind. John Force holds the record for the fastest

A Funny Car's entire body lifts up so crews can work on the engine. This is also the way the driver gets into the car!

Don "The Snake" Prudhomme is a legendary Funny Car driver who raced from the 1960s into the 1990s.

run in a Funny Car. He needed only 4.665 seconds to go from start to finish in a race in Joliet, Illinois, in 2004. That is less than a quarter of a second slower than Tony Schumacher's Top Fuel record. Force also set the record for the top speed in a Funny Car. His mark of 333.58 mph still stands. It is only about 2.5 mph slower than Schumacher's Top Fuel record.

Some of the most popular drivers in the history of car racing have been Funny Car drivers. John Force is one of them. Starting in the late 1980s, he became one of the greatest Funny Car drivers ever. He is still one of the best today! Force has won more national drag racing events than anyone else in history. In 1996, he became the first drag racing driver to be named the National Motorsports Driver of the Year. That honor usually goes to a NASCAR driver or an Indy car driver. From 1993 to 2002, Force won ten-straight season points championships in the Funny Car class.

Force turned 57 during the 2006 season, but he was still up near the top of the points standings. In fact, he is still so popular that he and his three Funny Car-racing daughters star in a reality television show called *Driving Force*. His daughter Ashley started entering NHRA Funny Car events in 2007. One day, dad and daughter might be racing against each other on the same track!

John Force has been a Funny Car superstar for more than two decades.

Anatomy of a Funny Car

The NHRA has certain rules about features that all Funny Cars must have. Here are some of those features:

• A Funny Car must weigh at least 2,300 POUNDS. Also, the front part of it must be at least three inches off the ground and the rest must be at least two inches off the ground.

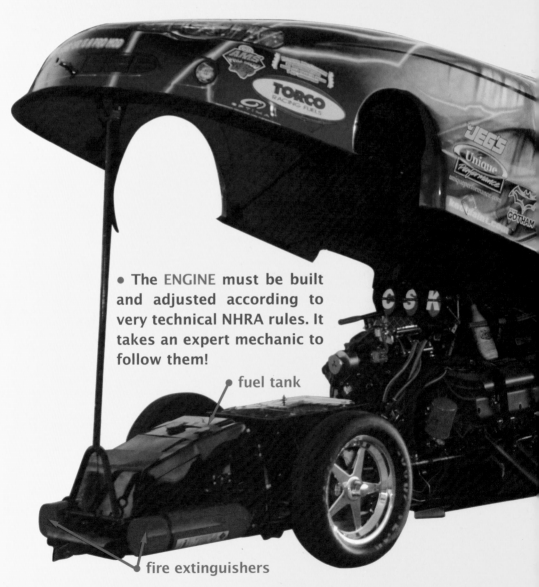

• The ENGINE must be built and adjusted according to very technical NHRA rules. It takes an expert mechanic to follow them!

fuel tank

fire extinguishers

• All drivers must be buckled into a SAFETY RESTRAINT (seat belt) system. They also must wear fireproof suits. All cars must carry a fire extinguisher. The underside of the car's body needs to have a special coating that will not burn. This gives the driver more protection if the car catches fire during a race.

• The outside SHELL must be made of graphite and weigh between 87 and 89 pounds. Much of the outer shell is just for show. It does not offer the protection that the outside of a regular car does.

• The large REAR SPOILER on the back of a Funny Car must be mounted on, not built in (as some are on regular cars). The rear spoiler forces air down on the rear tires and makes the car go faster.

• The back tires must be SLICKS that are 18 inches wide and 118 inches around. The front tires on a Funny Car are much smaller.

exhaust pipes

• The WHEELBASE must be between 100 and 125 inches. The wheelbase is measured from the middle of the front wheel to the middle of the back wheel.

In drag racing, women compete equally with men. That was not always the case. It was Shirley Muldowney who helped pave the way for today's women racers. Muldowney is a member of the Motorsports Hall of Fame. She was not the first woman driver in drag racing, but she is the most famous. Many people who do not even follow racing know her name.

"Cha-Cha," as Muldowney was called, made her mark in Funny Cars beginning in 1971. That year, she won her first major meet in a Funny Car. She moved to Top Fuel in 1974 and went on to win three NHRA season championships. She did it even though she faced many male drivers who did not think that a woman should be competing with men.

Today, women are still major competitors in all classes of drag racing. In fact, drivers such as Melanie Troxel and Hillary Will often qualify for the final 16 at Top Fuel drag meets. Ashley Force is expected to become a star one day on the Funny Car circuit, while Erica Enders is a popular Pro Stock driver.

Shirley Muldowney

CHAPTER 4

Pro Stock Racing

Many people would like it if their cars could go as fast as a dragster. But that would be dangerous—and against the law! Besides, regular cars are not built to race at the speeds of a dragster. A regular car could never handle that type of intense driving.

But if you go to an NHRA drag race or watch one on television, you might notice that some of the cars look a little like the cars

you see on the street. Are those regular cars? No—those are Pro Stock cars. Of all the drag racing cars, Pro Stock cars look the most like regular cars. The term "stock" means

Of all the drag racing cars, Pro Stock vehicles look the most like regular cars. This one is a Pontiac GTO, driven by Tom Martino.

that they are a regular automobile style. But of course that regular style has been modified, or changed, for racing.

For example, a Pro Stock car has a much more powerful engine than a regular car. These engines are also extremely expensive to build. In fact, the NHRA says that most Pro Stock engines cost more than $80,000 to build. That is a lot more than an entire passenger car costs, even with all the extras!

Another way that Pro Stock and regular cars differ is that most of a Pro Stock car's body is made of fiberglass, which is lighter than steel. Most of a regular car's body is made of steel.

Pro Stock cars are also different from other drag racing cars. For example, a Pro Stock car has a wheelbase of 99 to 105 inches. That is much shorter than a Top Fuel dragster. And unlike Top Fuel and Funny Cars, Pro Stock cars run on gasoline. But this is not ordinary gasoline—it is high-octane gasoline. All gasoline is given a number called an octane rating, which measures certain features of the gasoline. The higher the octane rating is, the better the car's engine performance will be.

There are strict rules for everything about a Pro Stock car. That includes its engine, its

brakes, and its weight. As in all classes of drag racing, NHRA officials inspect Pro Stock vehicles before and after every event. They need to make sure every driver is competing fairly.

The Best in Pro Stock

On October 15, 2006, Jason Line made the fastest run ever in a Pro Stock car. He raced the quarter mile in 6.558 seconds in his Pontiac GTO in Petersburg, Virginia. That same day, he set a new speed record of 209.75 mph. He broke the record held by Greg Anderson. Anderson is one of the top Pro Stock racers around today. He won the overall points championship four seasons in a row, from 2003 to 2006.

WILD FACT

Sometimes you might hear Pro Stock cars called "Factory Hot Rods." In other words, a Pro Stock car looks like a souped-up version of a regular passenger car that came out of a manufacturer's factory.

Greg Anderson celebrates his Pro Stock championship at the 2006 U.S. Nationals. It was his fourth championship in a row.

One of the best Pro Stock drivers of all time was Bob Glidden. He won the season points title an amazing ten times. From 1985 to 1989, he won the championship every year. Glidden usually was so much faster than everyone else that he had the fastest qualifying run in an amazing 23 races in a row during the late 1980s!

They Race Those?

Top Fuel, Funny Car, and Pro Stock are the most well known types of drag racing. But they are just three of more than 200 types of NHRA drag racing. Many do not even use cars. In fact, two more of the most popular types of drag racing use trucks and motorcycles.

Monster Truck Drag Racing

Imagine huge pickup trucks racing each other on a dirt track at 50 or 55 mph and crushing cars parked in their way. Yes, there are even drag racing competitions for Monster Trucks! Like at other drag-racing events, Monster Trucks race one-against-one. But these huge vehicles race on shorter tracks that are littered with obstacles, including cars, to run over and crush.

Motorcycle Drag Racing

Pro Stock motorcycles cover the quarter-mile track almost as fast as Pro Stock cars do. The fastest motorcycles go almost 200 mph. They usually cross the finish line in about seven seconds. The record is 6.940 seconds, set by Angelle Sampey in Reading, Pennsylvania, in 2006. Andrew Hines set the top speed record of 197.45 mph in Gainesville, Florida, in 2005.

CHAPTER 5

Race Weekend

The green light flashed, and Robert Hight was off in an instant. His Ford Mustang roared down the track at near-record speed. And yet, he could not seem to pull away from rival Whit Bazemore in the Funny Car final of the 2006 U.S. Nationals. "We went 328 miles per hour and it seemed like it took forever to get to the finish line," he said. But suddenly, it was over. "Forever" took 4.737 seconds, and Hight crossed the finish line

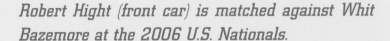

Robert Hight (front car) is matched against Whit Bazemore at the 2006 U.S. Nationals.

less than two-hundredths of a second faster than Bazemore. Hight was the U.S. Nationals champion!

Becoming the U.S. Nationals champion is a drag race driver's ultimate dream because it is drag racing's most important event. Football has the Super Bowl. NASCAR has the Daytona 500. And drag racing has the U.S. Nationals, nicknamed "The Big Go."

Drag racing fans from all over the country gather in Clermont, Indiana, on Labor Day weekend each year for four days of exciting racing at the U.S. Nationals. Clermont is just outside of Indianapolis, which is the most famous racing town in America. Men and women, old and young, travel to "Indy" for the U.S. Nationals.

In 2006, more than 80 competitors entered the Big Go in the three main race classifications: Top Fuel, Funny Car, and Pro Stock. After three days of qualifying, the field was narrowed down to the 48 fastest competitors (16 in each class).

Cover Your Ears!

If you ever go to a drag meet, remember that it is very important to protect your ears. Noise level is measured by decibels. The decibel level at a drag meet depends on how close you are to the cars. A Top Fuel dragster, for example, can pump out 120 decibels or more. By comparison, a jet engine at close range is 130 decibels. A rock concert is about 110 decibels. And normal conversation is only about 50 to 60 decibels. Anything over 85 decibels could damage your hearing over time. Wearing protective earmuffs is important.

Each year, the Nationals begin with qualifying runs in each class on Friday. This is a good time to get up close to the competitors and watch the crews in action. That is because they are not yet feeling the intense pressure of the final day of racing. They are more likely to spend time with the fans and answer their questions. Plus, this early in the competition, the crowds are not quite as big.

Before each run, the drivers do their burnouts. That means they spin their tires in a shallow puddle of water located close to the starting line. Spinning the tires heats them and cleans them for better traction on the racetrack. It also sends smoke into the air and gets the crowd going! The fans know a race is about to begin.

After each qualifying run, mechanics, also known as "wrenches," work like crazy in the garage. They are fixing leaks, checking fuel systems, servicing the engine—whatever needs to be done. Everything must be perfect for the next time the driver gets on the track.

Qualifying

Most events have two days of qualifying runs. But the U.S. Nationals is such a big event that there are three days of qualifying. By Labor Day on Monday, each class has been

WILD FACT

The area where drivers perform their burnouts is called the "Bleach Box." It contains only water, but it got its name because it used to contain bleach. That used to be the way drivers cleaned debris from the tires.

cut down to the 16 drivers with the fastest times. They race against each other in the first round of elimination races. The driver with the fastest qualifying time races against the driver with the slowest qualifying time. The second fastest driver races against the second slowest, and so on.

In the Funny Car class at the 2006 U.S. Nationals, John Force qualified for the top

As Top Fuel driver Morgan Lucas starts to fly off the starting line, the power of the engine lifts the front of his car off the track. The wheelie bar at the back keeps the car from flipping.

spot. His time of 4.691 seconds in his third qualifying run set a track record. He looked as if he had the most powerful Funny Car in the meet. But in his first-round elimination race against Jim Head, Force started way too early. He got a red light and was automatically disqualified. Suddenly, Force was out of the competition. Why? There are no do-overs in drag racing. It is "one and done" —one mistake and a driver is out of the competition. That is something else that makes drag racing such a thrilling sport.

Jim Head found that out the hard way two rounds later. He crossed the finish line first in a close race against Whit Bazemore. But Head was disqualified after his car touched one of the blocks in the center of the track. If any part of the car hits the blocks, it means it has gone into the middle of the track. And if a driver crosses into the middle of the track, he or she is disqualified.

Safety

In the second round of the Pro Stock elimination races, Ron Krisher had a terrifying crash. At top speed, his car drifted too far to the right. When he tried to adjust, the car went too far left. It crossed over the center of the track and rolled a couple of times.

Emergency crews were on the scene right away. The fire was put out, and Krisher was checked for injuries. He was lucky to walk away from the wreck with only a broken rib. Krisher's safety equipment did its job.

Safety is the biggest concern for the NHRA and its drivers and crews. If an accident happens, emergency workers are right on the spot. And a helicopter can quickly bring an injured driver to the nearest hospital if necessary. Just a few seconds' difference might save a life.

Pro Stock driver Ron Krisher was lucky to suffer only minor injuries after this crash at the 2006 U.S. Nationals. Emergency crews and safety equipment made all the difference.

Where Can I Watch?

The annual NHRA POWERade tour visits more than 20 cities in many parts of the United States. The 2007 season started in February with the Winternationals in Pomona, California. One month later, the drag racers stopped nearly 2,500 miles away, in Gainesville, Florida.

If you are not anywhere near a POWERade event on the NHRA main circuit, there are still plenty of local races to find. Check out NHRA.com for a list of tracks all over the United States. The Web site also lists the meets, special events, and regular shows on television each week. Even if you cannot make it to the track, you can still catch much of the excitement on TV.

The Winners

Sometimes, a driver knows his opponent has a more powerful or better-running car. In that case, the driver's best chance is to beat the other racer off the starting line. In fact, that is one of the few strategies drag racing drivers need to use to win a race.

For example, in the Pro Stock final at the 2006 U.S. Nationals, Dave Connolly knew that Greg Anderson had been running better times throughout the weekend. So he tried to take off faster at the green light. But he jumped too soon. Connolly got a red light and was disqualified. Anderson won the race, as well as the championship.

In Top Fuel, Tony Schumacher won his fifth U.S. Nationals Championship by beating Brandon Bernstein in the final. And in the Funny Car class, Robert Hight beat Whit Bazemore in that super-tight finish. As it is every year, the 2006 "Big Go" was a thrill for both drivers and fans.

Drag racing is a simple sport. Racers need to be the first off the starting line to shoot straight down a quarter-mile track and be the first to cross the finish line. But simple does not mean easy. These drivers have years of experience and know how to handle their powerful Top Fuel, Funny Car, and Pro Stock drag racing cars. They face danger in each race. And as in every sport, drag racing has many rules. But the strategy is simple: drive the fastest and win!

Ashley Force is ready for a Funny Car run at the 2007 Winternationals in Pomona, California.

Glossary

burnout—When a driver spins the wheels of his or her car in water to heat and clean them so they will better grip the track.

Christmas Tree—Electronic starting lights between the lanes of a drag racing track that signal the start of a race.

disqualified—No longer allowed to compete in the current race.

elapsed time (ET)—The time measured from the moment a dragster begins moving off the starting line until it crosses the finish line.

elimination race—Race at a drag meet in which the winner advances to the next round.

graphite—Soft, black mineral that is flexible but very strong. It is used to make the bodies of race cars. Its light weight will not slow down a dragster.

hatch—Opening in the roof of a Funny Car through which a driver can escape in case of emergency.

headers—Exhaust pipes that carry burned gas out of the engine.

nitromethane—Also called "nitro." Powerful fuel used in Top Fuel dragsters.

octane—A number rating assigned to measure certain features of gasoline. The higher the number, the better the engine performance.

qualifying run—A timed individual run on a drag-racing track, taken by each driver. The 16 drivers with the best qualifying runs get to compete in the elimination races.

spoiler—A device on the back of a Funny Car or Pro Stock car that directs air currents to improve the car's speed.

wheelie bar—Bar on the back end of a dragster that keeps the front wheels from lifting too far off the ground.

wrench—Nickname for a mechanic who works on a drag racing team.

Further Reading

Books

Dubowski, Mark. *Superfast Cars.* New York: Bearport Publishing, 2005.

Genat, Robert. *Top Fuel Dragsters.* Minneapolis: Motorbooks, 2002.

Pitt, Matthew. *Drag Racer.* Danbury, Conn.: Children's Press, 2001.

Sexton, Susan. *Drag Racing: Attacking the Green.* Des Moines, Iowa: Perfection Learning, 2003.

Internet Addresses

http://www.draglist.com A Web site that pulls together pictures, statistics, and stories from every kind of drag racing.

http://www.johnforce.com The official Web site of John Force, one of drag racing's most popular and successful drivers.

http://www.nhra.com The National Hot Rod Association's schedules, results, and driver profiles, plus a detailed history section.

Index